The Game Changer: A Captive Insurance Company

By

Don Deans and Joseph Tucciarone

Published by Don Deans and Joseph Tucciarone

300 South Oyster Bay Road

Syosset, New York 11791

Printed in the United States

Disclaimer

Table of Contents

Introduction....................v

Chapter 1: The Benefits of a Captive Insurance Company....................1

Chapter 2: Coverage and Policy Flexibility....................11

Chapter 3: Tax Benefit for Micro Captives: IRC Section 831(b)....................17

Chapter 4: Other Requirements for Micro Captives....................23

Chapter 5: Does It Make Sense for Your Client? The Feasibility Study....................29

Chapter 6: Nuts and Bolts I: Design and Implementation of the Captive....................37

Chapter 7: Nuts and Bolts II: Operations and Best Practices Going Forward....................45

Chapter 8: Wealth Creation, Preservation and Transfer....................51

Chapter 9: Pulling It All Together: A Real Life Case Study....................59

Appendix: Key Case Rulings and IRS Authority....................65

Introduction

game chang·er

noun: **game changer**; plural noun: **game changers**

> *an event, idea, or procedure that results in a significant shift in the current manner of doing or thinking about something.*

We have a game changer for your clients. It will impact what your clients *think and do* about:

- ✓ Risk management;
- ✓ Taxes;
- ✓ Wealth creation;
- ✓ Wealth transfer;
- ✓ Incentivizing key executives.

When you think "insurance" you don't normally think "game changer." But in this case, the phrase fits. The game changer? Captive Insurance Companies (referred to as captives or CICs) that are designed, implemented and operated specifically for small and medium sized businesses. For the most part, the benefits of CICs have been limited to Fortune 500 and other large companies – all of the Dow 30 and 80% of the Fortune 500 companies have CICs. The benefits of CICs are spreading to small and medium sized business because business advisors around the country like you are presenting the concept to their clients.

CICs have a history of providing benefits to their owners since the 1950s when Youngstown Sheet and Tube established the first CIC.

CICs are flexible entities that are made even better by electing special tax treatment under Internal Revenue Code Section 831(b). This election is available only to small CICs (also known as mini or micro captives) – those captives with less than $1.2 million in annual premiums. Such small amount of annual premiums will not work for a Fortune 500 company but is ideal for many, if not most, of your clients.

The bottom line is that we believe that almost all small and medium sized businesses will recognize tremendous business, risk management, tax, wealth creation (and wealth transfer) benefits by implementing a captive insurance company or CIC that elects IRC 831(b) tax treatment.

As the advisor, you will be the one that will bring this opportunity to your client's attention and drive the process. Once your client has expressed an interest in forming a captive we can assist with the feasibility study, design, implementation and operation of the CIC.

Who are we?
Independent Captive Associates, LLC:
A Game Changer

Independent Captive Associates, LLC has over 25 years of experience working with accounting firms and other professionals to assist their clients in creating and preserving wealth. We have experience in the formation of over 200 captives representing over 25 industries. Our focus has been to utilize the best of the best in the fields of law, accounting, captive management, investment expertise, property and casualty insurance and audit service. By creating independent standards, we ensure no link in the chain is weak. Each professional maintains a "five star" superior service. The collective management constantly oversees excellence and superior execution.

Visit us online at:
www.independentcaptiveassociates.com

Captives electing Section 831(b) treatment have special tax benefits that larger captives do not have. The Internal Revenue Service has provided guidance on how these entities must be set up and structured in order to take advantage of the tax benefits. Go to the Appendix for IRS rulings and guidance.

CICs electing Section 831(b) treatment is the focus of our book. Properly designed, implemented and operated, a CIC is primarily an alternative risk management tool that has several other significant tax, wealth creation and wealth transfer benefits.

Your client will need the assistance of experienced professionals to design, implement and operate their CIC if they hope to realize its game changing benefits. That is where we come in; *Independent Captive Associates, LLC (ICA)* is the experienced independent expert your client needs.

The first objection your client may have is that they don't have enough time in the day to run their current business, let alone run an insurance company. The time and attention that your client will have to devote to this process will be minimal because:

1. *He or she need not become an expert in designing, implementing and running the captive.* We bring the expertise needed. But as the advisor you will certainly want to be knowledgeable about CICs – the pros and cons. You want to know what questions to ask in order to protect your client from unethical promoters. This book will enable you to knowledgeably raise the topic with your client and work with us as we implement the CIC.

2. *Independent Captive Associates from ICA will also be able to handle the day-to-day operations of the captive,* (including all the compliance and regulatory issues) thereby minimizing your client's time commitment and leaving them free to run their business.

Most importantly, *the long term benefits of establishing the captive will far outweigh the costs.* Looking back a few years from now, your client will be very glad you brought this opportunity to their attention.

Demonstrating Value to Your Clients

In a competitive marketplace, isn't it important that your clients view you as a problem solver?

Aren't you always searching for ways to show your value to your clients? When you bring great ideas to the attention of your clients, won't they have a greater appreciation for your services? And won't these appreciative clients refer other potential clients to you?

What about creativity? Recommending that your client look into a CIC will give you an opportunity to demonstrate creativity to your client. It will show them that you are concerned about your clients, their ability to protect their family, their assets and their business. Before you hear "what can you do for me now?" from your clients, bring them the game changer – the captive insurance advantage.

If you believe we offer a game changing opportunity to your client, read on. If you believe this game changer will help you continue to demonstrate value to your clients, read on. If you don't believe us you risk your client hearing about the idea anyway, perhaps from a competitor.

Chapter One

The Benefits of a Captive Insurance Company

What you will learn: *Captive Insurance Companies (or CICs) are used by 80% of all Fortune 500 companies to help them manage risk. Increasingly small and medium sized businesses are discovering the benefits of CICs to help manage risk. CICs typically have common shared ownership with the companies they issue policies to or they may be part of a corporate group. There are many good business reasons for establishing a CIC. In addition to the tax benefits all insurance companies are entitled to, there are additional tax benefits for small captives (also referred to as micro captives) that have tremendous benefits for their owners. These tax benefits – which the taxpayer must elect – are found in Internal Revenue Code Section 831(b). In this chapter we discuss the general business, risk management and tax benefits of CICs. With this basic knowledge you will be better able to understand why many small and medium sized companies are establishing their own micro captives and electing Internal Revenue Code Section 831(b) tax treatment.*

Your clients, as business owners, understand risk. They live with it every day. It keeps them up at night. There are many different forms of risk.

There are, of course, the normal risks (but nonetheless real) of just being in business – drop in sales revenues, losing key customers, employees or suppliers, changes in consumer demand, changes in the regulatory environment, economic recessions – these risks *seems* endless and are rarely, if ever, covered by third party insurance. In addition there are other risks not directly related to your clients' business activity but that can be just as damaging if the risk turns into an occurrence. This includes damage to business facilities due to severe weather, liability for damage or injury caused by employees, computer hackers gaining access to important client data, misappropriation of money or inventory by dishonest employees and supply chain interruption (consider how many businesses depending on Japanese suppliers saw their business interrupted due to the tsunami of March 2011). Many times, your client's business is exposed to risks that the owner has not even considered but that may pose the danger of real loss depending on the circumstances, such as kidnapping and terrorism. Maybe the list of risks *is* endless, after all.

Most small and medium sized businesses deal with risk in one of two ways. Either they self-insure the risk or they shift the risk to an insurance company.

A business may decide to *self-insure* for a number of reasons. It may be unable to find an insurance company that will issue a policy covering a particular type of risk. Policies may be available but are too expensive. As a practical matter, the risk may be so small that self-insurance is the best answer. As we will explain later, the insurance market itself goes through periods when, for example, carriers pull out of a particular market because of an unexpected rise in claims or for other reasons. This, of course, can make it more difficult if not impossible to find certain types of coverage. Use of a captive can help businesses isolate themselves from these market cycles in the insurance markets.

Purchasing an insurance policy *shifts* all or a portion of the risk to the company issuing the policy. In effect risk is *distributed* among all the policyholders through their payment of insurance premiums (these concepts of *risk shifting and distribution of risk* will be especially important when we cover 831(b) captives). Some risks may have a very low probability of occurring (for example, destruction of a company's manufacturing facility due to a tornado) but if it does occur the loss is significant and can threaten the very existence of the business itself. In that case a traditional insurance policy may make sense. In some cases, risks that used to be shifted are now retained by the employer. For example, self-insurance of employee health care expenses of large employers has been in place for a long time. Lately, even small employers have self-insured a portion of such costs. This has been due, in part, to the rapid rise in cost of traditional policies.

Through use of a high deductible insurance policy, a business can reduce its premium costs by retaining a larger share of the risk. This may be an acceptable alternative if the higher potential cost of an occurrence to the business can be funded from current income or assets.

As you can see, how businesses manage risk is constantly changing due to both internal and external factors. As a business owner your clients must remain flexible and reconsider old assumptions about risk and how they will manage it.

If you think of managing risk as a spectrum – at one end is self-insurance, at the other end is purchasing an insurance policy to fully cover the risk, there are many ways to manage risk in between. *A CIC is a flexible entity that offers a hybrid way to manage risk that provides cost savings compared to traditional insurance and tax benefits not available if you self-insure.* In the next section, we will discuss why this is true.

Business Reasons are the Primary Reason to Form a CIC

There are very good *business* reasons to establish a Captive Insurance Company (CIC). These reasons apply as much to micro captives, such as your clients may wish to establish, as they do to large CICs created by Fortune 500 companies. This is important to understand because while large and small CICs do have certain tax advantages, the business reasons for establishing a CIC are greater than the tax advantages. In this case, the tax tail does *not* wag the dog. Tax benefits are important as are other reasons it makes sense to create a CIC – wealth creation and wealth transfer. We'll discuss those reasons later in the book.

Independent Captive Associates, LLC: A Game Changer

Use of *Independent Captive Associates* (ICA) early in the process of establishing a captive can mean the difference between success and failure. ICA will pull together the experienced team that will be key to all aspects of designing and implementing the captive.

One of the big business advantages of establishing a CIC is gaining greater control over risk management. When compared to purchasing traditional insurance, it can also save you money. The CIC tax advantages serve broader social purposes of providing incentives for business to better manage risk and achieve greater economic stability thus reducing overall insurance claims, as well as saving jobs (and tax revenues!). Good risk management is an important social goal. That is why the Internal Revenue Code provides tax incentives for insurance companies.

Here are some of the non-tax and tax reasons it makes sense to establish a CIC:

1. ***The CIC can tailor its coverage of your client's risks better than a commercially available policy.*** Your client's business may have unique coverage needs that cannot be met by traditional insurers. Alternatively, coverage from a traditional insurer may be available but too expensive or there are questions about whether the insurance company will continue to offer such policies. It is not unheard of for traditional insurers to stop providing coverage of certain risks and refuse to renew coverage. This leaves current policy holders vulnerable.

2. ***Cost savings can be significant.*** While premiums paid to the CIC must be calculated by an actuary such as ICA using appropriate standards, the premiums will be based on your client's company's more favorable claim history (if that is indeed the case) rather than the more unfavorable industry experience. In addition, the CIC will save on broker and agent commissions as well as insurer administrative costs and profits (in some cases, profits can be as much as 40% of the premium).

3. ***The CIC itself can shift some of <u>its</u> risk.*** The CIC will have access to the wholesale (as opposed to retail) reinsurance market. This is where insurance companies can buy insurance for themselves – shifting some of the risk they have taken on to another insurance company. Thus the term "reinsurance."

4. ***Greater control over payment of claims.*** Claims submitted to an insurance company (whether it is a third party insurer or a captive) must be paid based on the terms of the policy. It is not always clear, however, that a claim is payable under the terms of the policy. Investigations and ultimate payment of a claim (if warranted) will be completed with less red tape and the typical bureaucratic mind set and associated costs if the policy has been issued by a captive. Thus, the whole process of claim payments will be smoother and less adversarial.

5. ***For CICs large and small the premiums paid to a CIC are tax deductible.*** When a business self-insures, any money set aside in a special sinking fund or account to cover a potential loss is <u>not</u> tax deductible. When a business pays an insurance premium to an insurance company it is deductible as long as it is determined to be ordinary and necessary to the operations of the business. The IRS states: "To be deductible, a business

expense must be both ordinary and necessary. An ordinary expense is one that is common and accepted in your trade or business. A necessary expense is one that is helpful and appropriate for your trade or business. An expense does not have to be indispensable to be considered necessary." (from the IRS.gov website go to http://www.irs.gov/Businesses/Small-Businesses-&-Self-Employed/Deducting-Business-Expenses) As we proceed further into this topic keep the terms "ordinary and necessary" in mind. The value of a tax deductible premium payment depends on the tax rate imposed on the taxable income of a business (i.e., a tax deduction is worth more if the tax rate is 40% than if the tax rate is 20%). A $1,200,000 payment made to a separate account or sinking fund is not deductible until the loss actually occurs. A $1,200,000 premium payment made to a captive is tax deductible. At a 40% income tax rate (Federal and state) the tax savings is $480,000.

6. ***A CIC can become a profit center with increasing cash flow.*** While not the primary objective when created, over time a well-managed CIC can become very profitable and generate considerable cash flow. This is especially true if the CIC begins to expand its operations and pursues other underwriting opportunities which ICA can assist a captive to do. In addition, a well-managed CIC will have an increasing capital surplus which will provide other benefits including the ability to underwrite other risks or fund other projects. These benefits all accrue to the owners of the captive.

7. ***Your client retains complete control.*** At this point, one message should be clear – creating a CIC leaves your clients in greater control of their risk management efforts. With a CIC your client can insure risks previously covered by a higher cost commercial insurance policy or cover risks that were previously self-insured (of course, where it makes sense, your client can purchase or retain traditional policies to cover certain risks). Your client can also increase the deductibles on traditional policies, saving premium dollars while paying the deductible from a lower cost policy issued by the CIC. All of this gives the CIC owner greater flexibility in structuring its insurance program, as well as leverage when negotiating with an independent third party for insurance. That is, the CIC provides a source for coverage not previously available – and

when negotiating insurance rates, the owner can make that known to the insurance company.

8. ***There are other benefits associated with micro-captives we will discuss in detail later in this book.*** These include retirement planning, employee benefits, executive compensation, estate planning as well as asset protection benefits.

Independent Captive Associates, LLC: A Game Changer

One of the goals of establishing a captive is to increase the sponsoring firm's *efficiency*. Efficiency is the ability to produce a specific outcome with a minimum amount of waste, expense or unnecessary time or effort. An experienced and knowledgeable Independent Captive Associates consultant from ICA will create that efficiency for your clients.

Insurance Company Taxation

The insurance industry has extracted favorable tax treatment from Congress, as we will discuss in this section. As we stated above, there are broad social benefits to encouraging proper risk management practices among businesses. That is why the Internal Revenue Code provides a variety of tax benefits to insurance companies. Incentives are also provided to businesses to purchase insurance (self-insurance is not tax deductible, while premiums paid to an insurance company to insure the same risk are tax deductible).

We know what you are thinking and the question you have in mind.

The answer to your question is yes – we will be explaining the somewhat dry topic of insurance company taxation to you very briefly. No apologies – for you to introduce the tremendous benefits of CICs to your clients you need a basic understanding of the income taxation of insurance companies. We promise it will be relatively painless.

A CIC is a separate company that must elect to be taxed like a C Corporation. As a property and casualty insurance company it must file an annual tax return, Form 1120-PC U.S. Property and Casualty Insurance Company Income Tax Return. Don't worry, you won't have to buy the TurboTax version of Form 1120-PC. Preparation and filing will generally be overseen by the independent consultant you hire to run the day to day operations of your CIC.

Insurance companies are taxed under a special subchapter of the Internal Revenue Code: Subchapter L. It is here where the special tax benefits for insurance companies are found. But don't worry, you don't have to read it!

Large insurance companies take in millions (some take in billions) of dollars each year in premiums. These premiums can be thought of as the annual sales revenue of the company.

Normally, a company deducts current ordinary and necessary expenses from their gross revenue (in this case, premiums are a large part of an insurance company's gross revenues; they also report large amounts of investment income) to determine their taxable income. Simple enough, right?

In this case, the answer is no. Within each premium there is an amount that *may* eventually be paid sometime in the future to settle a claim. So, not all current premium income is taxable income - even though there is a mismatch between when the premium is received and when a legitimate claim is submitted for payment.

A portion of the current premium is *unearned* since it will have to be paid as a claim of unknown amount at some unknown time in the future. Legitimate claims that have been incurred but not yet presented are also known as Incurred-But-Not-Reported losses or IBNR.

This is where captives as well as other insurance companies receive a tax benefit unique to the insurance industry. Insurance companies are allowed to place some portion of the current premium income as a "reserve" against future claims that have yet to be reported. The "reserve" builds up over the years.

The ability of an insurance company to deduct the annual addition to its reserve from current premiums only *defers* income taxation. The income is not free. Like a deductible contribution to your 401(k) retirement account, income taxation is only deferred until you make a withdrawal from your account years later. But the tax deferral has real value since the contribution and earnings in the account grow tax deferred. Uncle Sam must wait for his cut. Similarly, the insurance company benefits from its tax deferral on current premiums.

All in the Family

For many years, the Internal Revenue Service fought the deductibility of premium payments made by one member of a corporate affiliated group of "family" to another member. This was the *"economic family doctrine."* After all, has the economic position of the entire group changed just because an amount of money (the premium) has gone from one member of the group to another? IRS resistance began to come to an end after the *Humana v. Commissioner* decision (refer to the Appendix for the citation). The Court held that the payments made by the subsidiaries would be deductible as insurance whereas payments made by the parent would not be. The IRS finally abandoned the "economic family doctrine" in Revenue Ruling 2001-31. In a series of subsequent Revenue Rulings the IRS changed its focus to providing safe harbors that taxpayers could use to make sure the captive was established in a way that would meet the risk distribution requirements of insurance companies (refer to the Appendix). This included Revenue Ruling 2002-89 providing a safe harbor that if met, allows premiums paid by the parent to the captive subsidiary to be deductible.

Annual additions to the reserve from current premiums are made not knowing the amount in claims that will ever be paid. If it turns out that additions to the reserve are larger than necessary, adjustments are made. The reserve is reduced and the amount of the reduction is taken into taxable income. *Again, additions to the reserve are not entirely tax free since a company making larger than needed additions to the reserve will eventually be taxed on the excess.*

But the special tax treatment of insurance companies and the deferral of income tax on a large portion of their premium income have tremendous value. Why do you think Warren Buffet, the famous investor, loves the insurance business? He loves the float, the use of the tax deferred reserves for many years before a claim is paid.

What You've Learned

CICs have tremendous value aside from their tax benefits. A CIC provides the business owner with greater flexibility and control over the risk management of his or her business. We provided a list of the nontax and tax benefits of a CIC. A significant tax benefit for both large and small businesses that establish and own a CIC is the tax deductibility of the premiums paid by the owner to the captive. When a risk is self-insured there is no deduction.

You also learned that insurance companies (not just captives) have special Federal income tax treatment. An insurance company is allowed to deduct from current premium income estimated amounts that may be paid in the future for claims.

In this chapter our discussion of insurance companies and CICs was general. The vast majority of Fortune 500 companies have captives. As discussed previously, there is also a special category of CIC that may make a special tax treatment election found in IRC Section 831(b). For these captives, its premium income is not just tax deferred; it is *tax free forever (even after it is withdrawn from reserves).*

In the next chapter we will consider the flexibility of the CIC. There is a long list of risks that your client can insure through a CIC. You will see some of the risks have always been present but inability to find a reasonably priced policy prevented your client from adequately insuring the risk. Now, with a CIC, these risks can be covered and better managed.

Chapter Two

Coverage and Policy Flexibility

What you will learn: *Before we get into details about 831(b) captives, let's consider the types of coverage that make sense for a CIC to offer. You will learn that in many cases, commercial insurance, self-insurance or some mix of the two may be perfectly acceptable. The key in this chapter is the flexibility that captives provide your client's risk management program. We provide only a partial list of possible coverages. The great advantage of the CIC is the flexibility it affords in the design and implementation of your client's risk management program. Each industry and every company has its own unique risk management needs. The CIC offers the flexibility needed to find an appropriate solution.*

Captives are used by hundreds of companies across many industries. They are very flexible, giving each business the ability to tailor its risk management program. In many (if not most) cases your clients are self-insured against unidentified risks without even knowing it. They only learn that a risk was self-insured when it materializes and is borne by the business.

Business related insurance policies issued fall into two major categories: *business liability* and *business casualty*. Business liability policies protect against claims made against the business by a third party. A business casualty policy claim is made by the insured business itself. Business casualty policies may be, according to some commentators, the best policy for a captive to issue. Liability policies can be broken down further:

Type of Business Liability Policy	Description	Comments
Direct	Pays third party making the claim; pays legal costs.	May not make sense for a captive. Creates an asset that the third party can go after.
Indemnification	Insured pays claims and asks for reimbursement from insurance company.	May make sense if policy is drafted correctly. Does not create an asset for the third parties to go after.

Litigation	Pays only for legal defense.	Good for captive to issue. Does not create an asset available to third parties.

Below is a partial list of the common types of insurance coverage that may be offered by a CIC:

- General liability
- Legal expense
- Deductibles
- Exclusions
- Employee health/benefits
- Cyber liability/security
- Professional liability/error and omissions
- Excess Errors & Omissions
- Environmental liability
- Contractual liability
- Excess environmental liability
- Employment practices
- Sexual misconduct
- Builders' risk
- Contractors' professional liability
- Mold
- Directors' and officers' liability
- Fiduciary liability
- Property damage
- Business interruption
- Supply chain interruption
- Auto liability
- General and umbrella liability
- Workers' compensation
- Labor shortage/strike loss reimbursement
- Employee dishonesty
- Patent infringement/Intellectual property
- Product recall
- Lender failure
- Business extortion
- Adverse weather and other natural occurrences (force majeur)
- FDA administrative actions liability
- Loss of key employee

- Loss of key customers
- Kidnapping
- Terrorism

Excess insurance on some coverage may also be appropriate for a captive to issue if there is a risk that losses may exceed the policy limits.

Captives give your client the ability to create highly customized policies with coverage that otherwise are not available in the commercial market. Many of your clients have unique risks that a captive can address.

In addition to having the ability to insure against a broader range of risks with a CIC issued policy, the owner gains greater control over many aspects of the policy. For example, if litigation results over a claim under a policy issued by an unrelated insurance company, the insurance company typically controls the attorneys and the course and resolution of the litigation although many insured parties would prefer to retain control over the attorneys and the course of the litigation. This may not be possible in a commercially available policy but is an easy provision to include in a policy issued by a CIC.

Youngstown Sheet and Tube Company

The modern CIC began in the 1950s. An insurance professional named Fred Reiss assisted Youngstown Sheet and Tube in securing insurance. Only a few large insurance companies competed for this business. With limited competition, premiums began to skyrocket. Working with Lloyd's of London, Fred came up with the first modern captive, Steel Insurance Company of America. Steel Insurance would issue an insurance policy to its parent, Youngstown. Lloyd's provided reinsurance to the new insurance company.

Where did the "captive" reference come from? In those days, many steel companies owned their own mines to make sure they had a steady supply of the raw materials they needed to produce steel. Known as "captive mines," Fred borrowed the term when he labeled the new insurance subsidiary a "captive."

Going back to the IRS definition of a deductible business expense we discussed in Chapter One – it must be "ordinary and necessary" to your client's business. Some of the types of coverage listed above may or may not represent potential losses to your client's business. Your client cannot just pick a risk and start a captive to provide coverage. For a physician group, mold is unlikely to be a concern and paying premiums for mold insurance would not be an ordinary and necessary business expense. On the other hand, malpractice suits are a great concern and if priced competitively, the premiums are a deductible expense when paid to a captive. By "priced competitively" we mean priced similarly to what may be offered in the commercial market, or that the price can be supported by an actuary using the appropriate actuarial standards. Ideally, the deductible premium paid to the captive is lower than that paid to an unrelated insurance company.

Many unethical captive promoters will assure business owners that they can insure against risks that, in reality, are extremely remote and not "ordinary and necessary" to the operation of the business. However, the policy must have some commercial reasonableness. Promoters anxious to sell the captive concept to business owners will also come up with premium payments that are many times larger than what would be available in the commercial market. These outsized deductions will also be challenged by the IRS. This is not to say that just because you have not purchased an insurance policy from a third party in the past to cover a risk you cannot form a captive to offer a policy. Just keep in mind the "ordinary and necessary" standard.

What is a valid insurance company?

A valid insurance company has a bona-fide business purpose; reasonable premiums; adequate capitalization and the operations of a true insurance company. When establishing a captive, keep these requirements in mind - do not focus solely on the tax benefits, rules and regulations!

But with those caveats in mind, there may be risks you currently self-insure where use of a captive may make sense.

Independent Captive Associates, LLC: A Game Changer

Know who your client is working with! Many captive promoters are not experts in captive formation and ongoing operation. They have little experience and may promise anything to obtain a client. Their advice often leads to a train wreck for your client. With our experience and market reputation, ICA will keep your clients on the right track.

Examples of when a Captive may make sense

Other coverage may make sense in a captive if, for example, the premiums paid are very close to the policy limits. Paying annual premiums of $40,000 does not make sense if the most that may be paid from the policy for a claim is $50,000. This brings up an important point – as part of the feasibility study to determine if a captive makes sense, your client will review current insurance policies and may find out that the premiums paid were much larger than claims paid over the years. This by itself is a good reason to conduct a feasibility study. Your client may be wasting tens of thousands of dollars each year in premiums paid to an unrelated insurer.

Another example is when your client manages certain risks covered by commercial insurance better than industry averages. A captive will price the premium closer to the actual risk your client is exposed to, taking into account the better risk management program.

Another CIC Benefit

If actual claims experience is favorable, the CIC will show a profit for the owner(s), which can be accumulated, distributed as dividends, or paid out to shareholders upon liquidation.

What You've Learned

Captives are a very flexible risk management tool. Flexibility extends not only to the types of coverage offered but includes the terms of the policy itself. Terms can be customized to the needs of your client. One example of maintaining control over a policy was greater control over litigation arising out of a claim. In many cases, clients may not even realize the extent to which they are self-insured for many risks. Unfortunately, your client only becomes aware of this when it is time for them to pay the claim.

CICs and the policies they issue can be used as an alternative to the commercial insurance market and self-insurance as a more cost efficient way to better manage any reasonable business risk.

In the next chapter, we will get into the details of the tax benefit available only to small captives - the IRC Section 831(b).

CHAPTER THREE

Tax Benefit for Micro Captives: IRC Section 831(b)

What you will learn: *In Chapter One we discussed the many benefits of owning your own insurance company – a Captive Insurance Company (CIC). We also introduced you to the tax advantages to which all insurance companies are entitled. Here is one more tax advantage – micro captives may elect alternative tax treatment under IRC Section 831(b). Companies making this election are limited to those with less than $1.2 million in annual premiums. Electing companies do not pay tax on their premium income, ever. It is more than just tax deferred, it is tax free income. By carefully explaining the history behind this tax benefit you will also appreciate that this is not an aggressive or questionable tax shelter. In fact, the IRS has issued guidance on the topic and at the owner's request, will issue a private letter ruling stating whether or not the micro captive is eligible to make the election.*

Recall that over 80% of Fortune 500 companies and all 30 companies that comprise the Dow Jones Industrial have CICs. The list of large companies that have captives includes well-known names such as Walgreens, The New York Times, Mars, Starbucks Coffee and Dunkin' Donuts. The fact that so many large companies use CICs has led many to believe that only large, international companies can benefit from CICs. As you've learned in Chapters One and Two, that is just not true.

Recognizing the importance of managing risk by obtaining insurance, Congress passed IRC Section 831(b) to give smaller and mid-size businesses an incentive to set up a CIC. This tax incentive will be the focus of Chapter Three. We'll review the history of the code section and explore in detail the code section itself. Not only will this provide you with the confidence to bring CICs to your clients' attention, but also understand that Section 831(b) is not a tax shelter or scheme. On the contrary it is a well-accepted risk management tool for businesses of almost any size.

IRC Section 831(b): Too Good to be True?

Sometimes the best way to understand a tax code section is by understanding its back story.

In the mid-1980s the property and casualty insurance market was in turmoil. It was, as insurance professionals refer to it, a "hard" market in which insurance premiums *increase* while the issuance of policies (or capacity) *decreases*. This dramatic period is now referred to as the liability insurance crisis.

As Born and Viscusi recount:

> *"Premiums soared, and there was widespread anecdotal evidence of major insurance disruptions. General liability and medical malpractice insurance were particularly affected by this surge in liability costs. During the crisis period, insurers reported policy losses well in excess of premiums. Insureds also began to experience substantial disruptions, as cases of denials of coverage...were highly publicized. The two-year period between 1984 and 1986 saw a concentrated surge in general liability premiums, which increased almost threefold. By almost any standard, the effect on the insurance market operations merited the "crisis" designation."* (Patricia Born and W. Kip Viscusi, Insurance Market Responses to the 1980s Liability Reforms: An Analysis of Firm-Level Data; The Journal of Risk and Insurance, 1994, Vol. 61, No. 2, 192-218).

In response to this crisis, Congress passed IRC Section 831(b) as part of the Tax Reform Act of 1986, providing a tax incentive to form micro captives. As we discussed earlier, insurance does play a valuable economic and social role. By passing IRC Section 831(b) Congress hoped to end the liability insurance crisis for small and mid-sized companies by giving them a way to avoid the roller coaster ride of the property and casualty insurance markets.

Thus, from the perspective of history this legislative background distinguishes IRC Code Section 831(b) from a tax shelter or scam. You can now better understand its utility and purpose and the benefit to your client and the marketplace. Of course, anytime there is an opportunity to create tax free income out of what is otherwise taxable income, the scammers and promoters will appear pushing the Code Section well beyond its intended purpose. Be very careful who you choose to work with in this area. Introducing a client to a promoter with ideas that only end up drawing IRS scrutiny will end up costing you a client...and possibly much more. Always keep in mind captive insurance is primarily an alternative risk financing tool. Tax benefits are certainly valuable and provide the incentive Congress intended when it passed the law. But tax benefits are secondary to the risk benefit purposes of CICs.

Now, let's dissect Section 831(b) and how it works.

Independent Captive Associates, LLC: A Game Changer

Our Independent Captive Associates consultants (ICCs) complement other professional advisors by presenting a wealth of experience different from other advisors in the market. ICCs possess a broad captive insurance perspective that is rarely matched. ICCs will bring value to your clients. Don't let your clients lose their focus and consider only fees – they must look at the value delivered.

The basics

IRC Section 831 is titled "Tax on insurance companies other than life insurance companies." The captives we are discussing are property and casualty insurance companies, not life insurance companies, so we are in the right code section.

Let's unpack this code section to understand how the captive can qualify for the special tax benefit.

IRC Section 831(b) is titled "Alternative tax for certain small companies." The alternative tax is found in Section 831(b)(1) taxing *only* the *"taxable investment income"* of the "small company" referenced in the title. Here it is – if the captive is a "small company" *only* its investment income will be subject to tax, *premium income will not be subject to tax.*

The next question is – what is a "small company" for purposes of the tax benefit? The definition of "small company" is found in Section 831(b)(2). The benefit applies if:

i. The net written premiums (or, if greater, direct written premiums) for the taxable year do not exceed $1,200,000, **and**

ii. The company elects application of this subsection for such taxable year.

Now you can understand where the $1,200,000 in annual premiums comes from. Unfortunately, the $1,200,000 amount is not adjusted annually for inflation. If the captive does not make use of the entire $1,200,000 annual premium ceiling, the unused portion may not be carried over to future years. We also learned that if there is no election, there is no tax benefit. Does the election have to be made annually? No – the code section goes on to say that the election "...shall apply to the taxable year for which made and for all subsequent taxable years for which the requirements of the clause (i) are met." In other words, in a subsequent year, if premium income exceeds $1,200,000, the tax benefit will no longer be available. In addition, once the election is made and the micro captive continues to meet the annual premium requirement, it can only be revoked with the permission of the IRS. The election itself is made on a "timely filed" Form 1120-PC.

How is "taxable income" defined? This is found in IRC Section 834 which is titled "Determination of taxable investment income." This tax calculation is made pursuant to Form 1120-PC and Schedule B to calculate taxable investment income of electing small companies-IRC Section 834. The taxable investment income is calculated on Line 21 and carried over to Line 2 on page 1 of the Form 1120-PC "Taxable investment income for electing small companies (Schedule B, line 21)."

Now, we don't expect many readers to actually pull out a Form 1120-PC and follow our instructions in the previous paragraph! So what was the point of providing the applicable IRC code sections and Form 1120-PC details? These details won't make you an expert by any means. But *it should give you and your clients the confidence that the tax benefits of micro captives are legitimate and grounded in the tax code as well as in the tax forms used by CICs to report their income subject to Federal income taxes.*

The IRS is concerned that CICs be used for their intended purposes and that the CIC is a legitimate insurance company taking on and distributing legitimate risk. A taxpayer may request (but is not required to request) a private letter ruling asking the IRS to essentially approve their captive's design, ownership structure and whether or not it is an insurance company.

We are often asked if it is possible for a controlled group of corporations to set up several small captives each entitled to the annual $1,200,000 tax free premium income. The answer is yes. *This is an area, however, where if multiple captives are required, care should be exercised and expert advice sought.*

In general, a controlled group may use more than one micro captive. If, however, there are multiple micro captives that are part of a consolidated return or member of a controlled group, the premiums of all the micro captives are aggregated together in order to determine if the $1,200,000 limit was exceeded. If this amount is exceeded, the election fails.

A controlled group may be either a *parent-subsidiary controlled group* or a *brother-sister controlled group* (for purposes of our discussion, we will ignore a third type, the "combined group").

If you look at IRC Section 831(b) closely you will notice that the definition of a "controlled group" for purposes of a micro-captive is different than the general rules governing controlled groups. IRC Section 831(b) looks to the definition of controlled group found in IRC Section 1563. IRC Section 831(b)(2)(B)(ii)(1) changes the definition of "controlled group" found In IRC Section 1563 *for purposes of micro captives*. The change lowers the 80% parent-subsidiary requirement of IRC Section 1563(a)(1) to just 50%. *With this change, it is the 50% ownership threshold and the brother-sister controlled group that becomes the primary focus of whether a controlled group exists.*

Without going into too much detail, if your client's goal is to create multiple captives that will insure members of a controlled group, with each captive entitled to the $1,200,000 annual limit, the ownership structure <u>*of the captives*</u> must be created carefully. Five or fewer parties must avoid owning more than 50% of more than one captive or those captives will be brought into the controlled group and their premiums aggregated for purposes of the annual limitation.

Here is an example:

Individuals	X Company	Y Company	Z Company	Captive 1	Captive 2
George	***25%***	***45%***	***30%***	100%*	0%
John	***35%***	***20%***	***30%***	0%	0%
Dolly	***20%***	***10%***	***20%***	0%	100%*
Maggie	***10%***	***25%***	***15%***	0%	0%
Unrelated parties	10%	0%	5%	0%	0%
Total	100%	100%	100%	0%	0%

***Ownership by the unrelated shareholders or their beneficiaries; see discussion of attribution rules below.**

In this example, X, Y and Z companies are part of the same brother-sister controlled group. Five or fewer individuals own more than 50%

of each company. If one or more captives were also part of the brother-sister controlled group, the $1,200,000 annual limit would apply in the aggregate to those captives.

The goal would be to make sure the captives are owned in such a way so that they are not part of the controlled group. That way, each captive would maintain its own $1,200,000 limit *even if all the captives insure the same corporate group.* In the example above, the captives are owned 100% by separate individuals so the captives are not included in the controlled group.

Think of it as buying insurance from unrelated insurance companies (which is what the captives are if ownership is structured properly). Your client does that now! In the case above, however, the captives would not be considered as part of the brother-sister controlled group.

Also keep in mind, the IRS can attribute ownership and control of stock held by spouses, children under age 21 and by companies or other entities, including trusts, of which your client owns 5% or more. This attribution can trip up your client's ownership structure and find a controlled group where none was thought to exist.

Again, use of multiple captives is a complex area that requires expert advice.

Chapter Four

Other Requirements for Micro Captives

What you will learn: *To benefit from establishing a micro captive insurance company, the relationship between your client and the micro captive must constitute "insurance." As a basic matter, insurance must cover an insurable risk and for purposes of the Internal Revenue Code, the premiums paid for a policy covering an insurable risk is deductible only if the risk is a reasonable business risk that is an ordinary and necessary part of doing business. Further, insurance only exists if (i) risk is shifted by the insured to a properly licensed and operated insurer (in this case the micro captive) and (ii) the insurer distributes that risk to third parties by issuing insurance policies to them and collecting the related premiums (or by reinsuring the risk which we discuss later). The insurer must distribute the risk among a sufficient number of other insureds so that any one claim by one policyholder is unlikely to bankrupt the insurer. In this chapter you will learn about risk shifting and risk distribution. In addition, you will learn about other requirements that a captive must meet in order for the owner to recognize all the benefits of creating a micro captive. Some of the requirements are not tax related, such as the proper licensing of the insurance company. Other requirements are tax related - the IRS has issued several Revenue Rulings on what constitutes risk shifting and risk distribution. The IRS has also issued guidance on the proper ownership structure of a micro captive.*

Placing too much emphasis on the tax issues surrounding micro captives may result in losing sight of the other factors that go into implementing a successful insurance program. That is a mistake because if your only goal is to capture the tax benefits of a micro captive insurance program your effort will most likely fail.

Keep in mind you are implementing a program of insurance using a property and casualty insurance company. That means:

1. There must be a reasonable, existing business risk.

2. There must be a properly operated and licensed property and casualty insurance company.

3. There must be actual insurance, meaning:

    a. The risk must be *shifted to* the property and casualty insurance company; and

    b. The captive must properly *distribute* that risk to third parties by reinsuring the risk or issuing insurance policies to and receiving premium payments from, third parties).

4. The micro captive must operate as a separate company from its owner.

If any of these elements do not to exist, the benefits of the micro captive will be lost. Let's look at these one by one.

There must be a reasonable, existing business risk

In Chapter Two we provided a long list of coverages that can be provided by micro captive insurance coverage. Coverage provided must have some business reasonableness. Alien abduction insurance will most likely fail IRS scrutiny. Such a policy is neither *ordinary nor necessary* to the business as required by IRC Section 162 which governs which business expenses are deductible for Federal income tax purposes.

Even a "plain vanilla" general liability policy offered by the micro captive that costs many times what is available through a commercial policy will also fail IRS scrutiny. While the type of policy may be both ordinary and necessary, the premium charged is not and the excess of premium over the commercially available rate will not be deductible. This is true unless it can be proved that the insurance contract was not plain vanilla. Recall that one of the benefits of establishing a micro captive is that the terms of the policy may be customized for the needs of the insured more so than a commercial policy. These customized policy provisions may justify a higher premium than that paid on a commercial policy.

To determine types of coverages that will be offered and pricing, you may start with a review of your client's current coverage through your existing commercial policies. But you are by no means limited to just existing coverage. This is where the assistance of a knowledgeable, independent captive consultant can help. He or she should be able, along with an actuary to identify the types of coverages that may best be offered through a micro captive. The actuary will also assist with the pricing of the policy depending on the type of coverage as well as the terms of the policy. All of this will be done as part of creating the business plan and the feasibility study. Ultimately, of course, all of these tasks will be performed by, or on behalf of, the captive itself once it is established and licensed. After all, as an insurance company, the mangers will be responsible for underwriting, claim and financial management, compliance and reporting (but may outsource these functions to an independent servicing company).

There must be a properly operated and licensed property and casualty insurance company

The IRC Section 831(b) election for micro captives is available to "...every insurance company other than life..." that meets the annual net written premiums limit (equal to or less than $1,200,000) and elects the tax benefit of such section. That is why, earlier in this book, we mentioned that a captive is a property and casualty company, it cannot issue life insurance policies. Insurance companies – whether life or property and casualty - must be properly licensed as such in the state or foreign country in which they are *domiciled*. We will discuss licensing and domicile in a later chapter. Suffice it to say, licensing is necessary, but by itself is not adequate to cause a captive to be recognized as an insurance company by the IRS.

IRC Section 831(c) provides that for purposes of Section 831, "insurance company" has the meaning given to the term in Section 816(a). Section 816(a) states that an insurance company is any company of which *more than half of its business* during the taxable year is the issuing of insurance, annuity contracts or the reinsuring of risks underwritten by insurance companies (i.e., premium income must exceed investment income). Otherwise neither the IRC nor regulations define property and casualty insurance.

Proper licensing also reaches the initial capitalization of the insurance company as well as its surplus requirements. These requirements are set by the laws of the domicile in which the insurance company is licensed. We discuss these issues more in the chapter on the nuts and bolts of establishing a captive.

For the IRS to recognize a micro captive as an insurance company, there must be (of course) insurance. Insurance only exists if there is *risk shifting* as well as *risk distribution*. That discussion is next.

Insurance requires *risk shifting* and *risk distribution*

Simply put, risk shifting is what the insured does, while risk distribution is what the insurer does.

Whether or not there is an actual shifting of risk can be a point of contention between the IRS and the taxpayer. Determining if risk has been shifted is part art, part science. In general, if risk has been shifted, the insurance company has the potential of suffering a loss depending upon the terms of the policy. In Revenue Ruling 2005-40, the IRS provided that:

> "Risk shifting occurs if a person facing the possibility of an economic loss transfers some or all of the financial consequences of the potential loss to the insurer, such that a loss by the insured does not affect the insured because the loss is offset by a payment from the insurer."

Policies issued that are similar to policies issued by other companies in the industry can bolster the argument that risk shifting has taken place. So can the use of independent experts to make sure the captive is operated like an insurance company.

Seems simple enough, but the IRS will scrutinize the terms of the policy with the micro captive to make sure that the risk is really transferred and there are no provisions that put the final burden of loss on the insured. In such a case, the arrangement is not insurance with deductible premium payments. The IRS would argue the arrangement is one of self-insurance absent a shifting of the risk. Payments made to a reserve fund set up as part of a plan of self-insurance, of course, are not deductible for tax purposes.

Risk distribution is what insurance companies do. Revenue Ruling 2005-40 also defines risk distribution:

"Risk distribution incorporates the statistical phenomenon known as the law of large numbers. Distributing risk allows the insurer to reduce the possibility that a single costly claim will exceed the amount taken in as premiums and set aside for the payment of such a claim. By assuming numerous relatively small, independent risks that occur randomly over time, the insurer smoothes out losses to match more closely its receipt of premiums."

The Revenue Ruling goes on to state: "Courts have recognized that risk distribution necessarily entails a pooling of premiums, so that a potential insured is not in significant part paying for its own risk."

Think about that last statement - a captive owned 100% by its parent and that insures the risks of only its parents is not an insurance company. It is not distributing its risks. The parent is "...in significant part paying for its own risk."

Risk can be distributed in a number of ways – by insuring a large number of clients, by insuring for different risks (auto, homes, boats, motorcycles, crops, etc.) and insuring across different geographic areas. The point is – an insurance company distributes risk. No distribution of risk, no insurance.

We will discuss how a micro captive can distribute its risk in order to meet this definition of risk in the chapter on the nuts and bolts of establishing a captive.

The micro captive must operate as a separate company from its owner

There is a long standing legal principle that a court must, in general recognize the separate nature of a company even if that company is part of a larger corporate family. This provision affects not only insurance payments from a parent (or one of its subsidiaries) to a captive. Every day, there are thousands of transactions as goods are bought and sold among corporate members of the same families. These are recognized as legitimate business transactions because companies within the same corporate group are recognized as distinct entities. Intercompany pricing is used to establish the prices at which the transactions will take place.

Similarly, the micro captive selling insurance to its parent or to the other subsidiaries in a corporate group is recognized as a distinct business entity. But this recognition comes only if the micro captive operates as a separate company. Accounting records must be kept separate; there should be no overlapping of management and personnel. Premiums must be arms' length and established using acceptable actuarial standards. For all purposes the captive must appear and operate as a separate company. It must be capitalized sufficiently and maintain adequate reserves to pay its claim (in the first instance this will be determined pursuant to rules issued by the relevant state or foreign insurance commissioner). It must issue valid and enforceable contracts to its parent and other members of the corporate group.

The IRS provides a statement in Revenue Ruling 2002-89 on what is necessary for the parent and subsidiary to be seen as operating independently:

> "The amounts P(arent) pays to S(ubsidiary) under the arrangement are established according to customary industry rating formulas. In all respects, the parties conduct themselves consistently with the standards applicable to an insurance arrangement between unrelated parties. In implementing the arrangements, S may perform all necessary administrative tasks, or it may outsource those tasks at prevailing commercial market rates. P does not provide any guarantee of S's performance, and all funds and business records of P and S are separately maintained. S does not loan any funds to P."

What You've Learned

Establishing and benefitting from a captive insurance company means meeting both tax and non-tax requirements. We focused on several requirements including the shifting and the distribution of risk, making sure the captive is a properly licensed insurance company, and that it operates as such. Finally, it must be established and operated as a separate company from its parent and other subsidiaries in the corporate group.

Next up, we will look at the feasibility study – does a micro captive make sense for your client?

Chapter Five

Does It Make Sense for Your Client? The Feasibility Study

What you will learn: *Setting up a micro captive can be an expensive and time consuming process – if there are not sufficient economic and risk management benefits to your client. If the benefits are there, the costs and time expended will be well worth the effort. A feasibility study will include a detailed analysis to help your client determine the potential benefits of a captive strategy. In addition to the feasibility analysis, there will be an actuarial study and a business plan with pro forma financial statement. If completed by an experienced, independent advisor, the study will provide objective guidance to your client's question "will establishing a captive serve to improve my business' risk management strategy and help build, preserve and transfer wealth?" In this chapter we will look at the essential elements of a feasibility study and other tools that will help your client make a decision.*

The successful implementation and ongoing operation of a captive insurance company starts when you assemble your advisory team. This cannot be over emphasized – many captive advisers and promoters will claim knowledge and experience but very few have a successful track record they can point to. The advisory team should be assembled as early in the process as possible.

Implementation and ongoing management of a captive is accomplished by your client's team. The team typically includes attorneys, actuaries, insurance professionals, a CPA, a tax professional (a tax attorney or CPA), an investment advisor and the manager of the captive's day to day operations. The final makeup of the team will depend, in part, on the laws of the domicile chosen for licensing. Finding and assembling a team is difficult. Making a disparate and independent group of professional advisors work together is nearly impossible. Too often, professionals work in their individual "silos," communicating poorly (if at all) with the other professionals.

The solution is to work with a knowledgeable, experienced advisor with an extensive track record of success. The advisor will have overall responsibility to hire and manage the team.

Before your client begins the process

More than likely, your client has asked him- or herself one or more of the following questions recently:

1. Do I have a serious risk that could impact my business operations? That could destroy what I have created? Maybe the loss of a key customer, a large legal expense or disruptive changes in government legislation?

2. How do I protect the assets that I have created? I am a target. We live in a litigious society, how can I protect what I have worked so hard to create?

3. There must be a way of creating additional tax deferrals and perhaps even a conversion strategy? Why are so many wealthy people paying so little in tax and my rate is so high? What do they know that I don't?

4. How do I pass on what I have created to my family? How can I enhance my future estate planning? The government taxes are onerous. Most family businesses won't last more than a couple generations!

5. I am at the mercy of the banks. How can I create an inexpensive source of capital? Where do I access capital at favorable rates to expand and not burden my business?

Clients asking these questions are good candidates for a micro captive insurance company. But beyond these questions are a number of factors that must be considered before the design phase begins.

For example, good candidates for establishing a captive generally meet one or more of the following criteria:

6. $10 million in gross revenue

7. $500,000 or more in operating profits

8. Stable cash flow

9. Substantial self-insured/uninsured business risk

In addition, a suitable candidate is a business seeking substantial annual adjustable tax deductions and/or with multiple entities or businesses that can create multiple operating subsidiaries.

In addition to having an experienced captive advisor from the beginning of the process, another key to running a profitable captive is to identify and insure risks that are legitimate but have a low probability of occurring. This is because risks that have a high probability of occurring would inhibit the ability of a captive to help achieve the owner's or owners' other financial goals. A good accredited actuary should be able to identify risks that meet the criteria.

Design, Licensing, Formation, Compliance, Management

The process we describe below from design to ongoing management of the captive should be done with one thing in mind: efficiency. Efficiency is the ability to produce a specific outcome with a minimum amount of waste, expense or unnecessary effort. Efficiency is an outgrowth of experience. Work with an experienced advisor.

There are five major steps involved in getting a successful captive up and running. Under each major step there are several other key tasks that the captive advisor must be able to assist your client with:

1. **Captive Design**

    - Insurance coverage and risk analysis
    - Business entity and captive formation design
    - Feasibility study, business plan and pro forma financial statements
    - Insurance coverage design and premium assessment
    - Domicile selection

2. **Formation**

    - Incorporation and legal advice
    - Selection of actuary, auditor and tax preparer

3. **Licensing**

    - Insurance license application assistance
    - Insurance jurisdiction approval

4. **Regulatory Compliance**

    - Captive insurance company accounting and records set up and maintenance
    - Preparation of quarterly financials
    - Investment management or active liaison with investment manager
    - Regulatory reporting
    - Annual audit

5. **Ongoing Management**

    - Draft and issue insurance policies
    - Claims management
    - Annual risk coverage analysis
    - Ongoing coverage assessment
    - Purchase of reinsurance

The Feasibility Study

Forming a captive, if done correctly, means forming a valuable new asset for your client. As we discuss elsewhere, while the primary purpose of a captive is risk management, it can also serve as a generational wealth accumulation, transfer and preservation tool. That is why it is so important to get it right from the beginning. The captive landscape is littered with the bodies of captives that were poorly advised from the start. This is why a good feasibility study is so important.

The goal of the *feasibility study* is to determine if your client's business and establishing a micro captive is a good fit. It will address many issues – from the anticipated rate of return to clarifying which risks the captive should insure. More practical considerations such as claims processing adjudication and payment as well as a plan for ongoing captive management will also be part of the study. An actuarial report will be included that identifies risk-financing needs and estimated premiums.

A feasibility study can take up to 12 weeks to complete. It may take longer depending upon how many individuals are involved reviewing the study. Some of the delay can be attributed to the amount of data that must be gathered – quicker turnaround times for data requests can shorten the time it takes to complete the study. The owner will need to provide loss information and other financial information to the actuary. Prepare your client early on regarding the demands that will be made for information. Responding to such requests should be given high priority.

Most U.S. domiciles require a feasibility study. It helps assure the regulators that owner has done some due diligence before making a decision on moving forward with establishing the captive. While internal staff of the future parent or owner of the company may do the study, it is rare that a company's staff has the requisite knowledge and experience. While a feasibility study can be undertaken by anyone, it is best if an experienced, independent risk management advisor is in charge.

A properly completed feasibility study will explain clearly how the captive will accomplish what it is designed and expected to do. Information on the structure, capitalization, premium income, costs, loss control, claims payment, etc. will be included.

In addition to the feasibility study itself, the study may include the following:

1. An actuarial study;

2. A business plan;

3. Pro forma financial statements.

We will briefly describe each element of the study. Keep in mind, each feasibility study and accompanying documents is slightly different, so it may not contain all the elements listed below or it may contain other items not listed.

Actuarial study – The actuarial study will form much of the basis for both the feasibility study and the business plan. The actuarial study will include information on the risk(s) to be insured along with:

- Premium determination;
- Coverage limits;
- Underwriting policy;
- Reinsurance plan,
- Surplus contribution and withdrawal policy;
- Loss control policies; and
- Claims processing.

Not all jurisdictions require an actuarial study to be performed. Even if not required, an actuarial study may speed up the licensing process. It will also be helpful should the IRS review the transaction to determine the business reason for establishing the captive and whether the premium is an "ordinary and necessary" business expense.

The feasibility study may also review what domicile alternatives are available and which may be the best candidates. The domicile is the jurisdiction in which the captive will be licensed. This may be in a state (such as Vermont or South Carolina) or in a foreign jurisdiction such as Bermuda. A final decision may not be made until the decision to move forward is made. Here is another reason you will want your advisor to be independent – you want to make sure the domicile you select is the one best for your client, not the one the advisor may have financial or other ties to.

Once the feasibility study is completed and the decision is made to move forward with formation and implementation of the captive, an application for an insurance license must be submitted to the Insurance Commissioner in the domicile of choice. We will cover this step in the process in the next chapter on the nuts and bolts of captive design, formation and implementation.

Of course, the feasibility study may determine that forming the captive is not in the best interests of your client. While disappointing, it is better to find that out early in the process rather than moving ahead without a feasibility study only to find out that thousands of dollars and hundreds of hours of time were wasted.

Business plan – The feasibility study is a somewhat narrowly drawn document focusing on the risk management aspects of the captive and whether it is feasible. The business plan is a broader document looking at the actual implementation of the plan and how it will operate over the next several years including an overview of plan management (including outsourced functions) and operations. At its heart is explaining how the captive will conduct its business – the business for which it hopes to be licensed. There will be a description of the captive, ownership structure, management, governance (the Board of Directors) and capitalization. Also included will be detail regarding captive operations and a list of local professionals who will be providing services to the captive. Details on upper management who will be running the everyday operations will also be included.

Attachments will include some or all of the following:

- The articles of incorporation
- Bylaws
- Organizational charts
- Investment policies

Pro forma financial statements – A multi-year (usually five) projection of the basic financial statements, income, balance sheet, sources and uses of cash, impact on parent's consolidated earnings.

What You've Learned

The success or failure of a captive may be determined before the license application is ever submitted! The question is: is there a good fit between the benefits a captive can provide and your client's business and risk management needs? A carefully written feasibility study along with an actuarial study and a business plan can lay the groundwork for a successful micro captive strategy.

In the next chapter we will consider some other important factors in the design and implementation of a micro captive including domicile, captive structure issues and day to day operations.

Chapter Six

Nuts and Bolts I: Design and Implementation of the Captive

What you will learn: *Once the decision is made to move forward with a captive, final decisions have to be made regarding ownership, structure, domicile, capitalization, investment policy and reinsurance. All these topics are interrelated – the decision made regarding ownership will affect the structure. The decision made regarding domicile will affect capitalization and investment policy. In this chapter, we discuss these important issues. In addition, the objective of establishing the captive must also be kept in mind. A captive that will also be used to preserve and transfer wealth will be designed differently than one where that is not a primary goal. Because of the complexity involved, it is best if your client uses an experienced adviser to work through and help resolve each topic.*

If, based on the feasibility study and other factors we discussed in the last chapter, it makes sense for your client to move ahead with establishing a micro captive, the next step is to make decisions regarding:

- Ownership
- Structure
- Domicile
- Capitalization
- Investment policy
- Reinsurance

We will briefly discuss each topic. Keep in mind, however, that each of these topics is complex and interrelated. For example, a decision on ownership will impact the structure of the captive while a decision on the domicile in which to become licensed will impact capitalization as well as the license application process. This is another reason to use an experienced, independent and knowledgeable adviser. He or she must understand how a decision made with regard to one topic will affect the decisions made with regard to other topics. In some cases, a decision with regard to one topic will limit the alternatives available with regard to another. It is important that the adviser be able to take a broad view when it comes to the design and implementation of your client's captive. Only in this way can you ensure that your client's objectives in establishing the captive will be met.

Ownership

In many cases, the owner of a captive is the parent corporation of an affiliated group. The subsidiaries are typically operating companies. This type of arrangement is referred to as a "pure captive" or a "single-parent captive." The captive in this case has just one owner.

The operating companies are referred to as brother-sister corporations. The captive is a member of the affiliated group and is also considered a brother-sister corporation. Premium payments by the brother-sister corporations to the captive are deductible (if they are considered "ordinary and necessary" business expenses, meet the requirements of insurance we discussed earlier, and satisfy the "risk distribution" test of distributing risk among a suitable number of insured parties). Any insurance premium payments made to the captive by the parent are not tax deductible (unless the safe harbor of Revenue Ruling 2002-89 are met (also see Revenue Rulings 2002-90 and 2002-91)). This arrangement is seen primarily with large publicly traded companies. Obviously, large publicly traded corporations would have little use for a micro-captive with its annual limit on premiums at $1,200,000.

On the other hand, a micro captive may fit a small or medium sized business very well. These businesses will have other objectives in mind when establishing a micro-captive. In addition to its benefits as a risk management tool, the micro-captive may be an excellent wealth preservation and transfer tool. In this case, other ownership arrangements are used. If the business owner's purpose for establishing the captive is wealth preservation and transfer, the owner of the captive may be a trust for the benefit of his or her children. Such captives are known as a closely-held insurance company or CHIC. We will discuss use of a captive for wealth transfer in a subsequent chapter.

Structure

The structure of the micro-captive can take any one of several forms in addition to the simple parent-subsidiary or pure captive mentioned above. In this section we will discuss several possibilities. Our purpose here is not to provide you or your client with a comprehensive treatment on this topic. We've given you enough in the discussion below to help you understand that captives come in many shapes and sizes. An independent adviser can help your client select the structure that best meets their needs and will help them accomplish their goals.

A captive domiciled in the United States may be a stock, mutual or Limited Liability Company, or reciprocal insurance company (a type of nonprofit). Offshore captives are usually stock or mutual companies. In each case the captive must elect to be treated as a C Corporation.

Moving away from the single parent or pure captive is typically done when separate businesses have a common interest in better risk management. Separate but similar businesses often have homogenous risks and may find it advantageous to join together as a way to better manage risk at a lower cost. A good example of that is a *Risk Retention Group (or RRG)* which is a form of *group captive.*

A *group captive* is one that underwrites the risks of individuals or businesses that are members of an organization or association or have similar (homogeneous) business risks. There are several forms of group captives including association or industry captives. You'll notice that a group captive will sell insurance to several different businesses - more than would a single-parent captive.

That is because when a captive is licensed in its domicile of choice, the license is a *restricted non-life insurance license.* The captive cannot sell life insurance. In addition, a captive does not have a general insurance license to sell policies to third parties. This restriction does not mean the commissioner is any less concerned about the captive's reserves and ability to pay claims.

An RRG is created to insure similar risks for its owners. Once licensed in one state it can operate in any other state without being licensed. It was established via Federal law through the Federal Liability Risk Retention Act (LRRA). The LRRA, for the most part, exempts the RRG from state laws. Policyholders are also members of the RRG and share in profits (if any). Like any captive, it gives owners an incentive to better manage the risk insured by the RRG since they all directly benefit from these efforts by sharing in the profits.

Other popular structures include:

- *Agency captives* are owned by insurance agents or brokers;
- *Branch and sponsored captives* are used when a foreign captive cannot insure a risk, such as employee benefit risks that are governed by ERISA (the Employee Retirement Income

Security Act), so it sets up a U.S.-based captive of its own;

- *Physician groups* are formed by large groups of doctors who, on their own, have practices that are too small to attract much attention from reinsurers (companies that sell insurance to other insurance companies that wish to reduce their risk exposure are referred to as reinsurers). While a small physician group may not attract interest from a reinsurer (the annual premium would be too small) a larger group of physicians may join together to form a captive. This captive will offer a reinsurer enough premium dollars to gain their attention.

There are other structures such as segregated cell companies that are used by single parent captives, group captives and so-called rental captives. A segregated cell captive is attractive because it may reduce the capital requirements and offer better bankruptcy protection.

Our purpose here is to help you understand that micro-captives come in several shapes and sizes. Even a rudimentary understanding of the various structures available will help you ask questions of the adviser and better understand the response.

Domicile

A domicile is where the captive is formed and licensed as an insurance company. Once licensed as an insurance carrier, the captive may apply to be an admitted carrier in any other jurisdiction. As a practical matter, most states allow a brother-sister subsidiary to purchase insurance from the captive (also a brother-sister subsidiary) without the captive having to become licensed.

A domicile may be one of many states in the U.S. that offer licensing for captives, or an offshore (foreign) domicile. Years ago, captives typically selected offshore domiciles rather than states. Once the states caught on to how lucrative it was to offer restricted insurance licenses to captives, many began to pass captive legislation. In addition to various licensing fees and annual fees, the states charge premium taxes calculated as a percentage of premiums paid to the captive. This can quickly add up to a substantial amount going into state coffers each year. Starting with Vermont in 1981, other states, such as South Carolina, soon followed. Now the majority of states offer favorable captive legislation and licensing. Many of them market their services aggressively. Captives mean not only fees and premium taxes paid to a state but jobs and insurance company funds deposited in local financial institutions. Most advisors believe that having a domestic domicile makes sense unless there are overriding reasons to seek out a foreign domicile.

The advantages of a domestic domicile include no tax reporting of a foreign entity, lower formation and ongoing costs (in some cases – your adviser should compare the formation costs of the states being considered over the offshore domiciles), convenience and lower costs reaching the domicile should a trip be required, and better service from the state bureaucracies. Also, keep in mind that some structures (such as the RRG described above) must have a domestic domicile.

The advantages of a foreign domicile vary, but can include access to foreign investments that may not otherwise be available to a domestic domiciled company. There also may be some tax advantages and additional asset protection benefits. You should review these topics with the adviser.

IRC Section 953(d) Election

An offshore captive may make an Internal Revenue Code Section 953(d) election which will tax the captive as a U.S. corporation. Most captives make this election for a variety of reasons. Because of this election, there is little in the way of a tax advantage for an offshore captive.

While selecting the domicile is important, the increase in competition among the states and foreign countries for captives has been a real benefit to captive owners. The need to stay competitive means jurisdictions tend to match the legislation of their competitors. Your adviser should provide you with guidance as to which domicile best fits your client's needs.

Capitalization

Capitalization means money the owner must come up with in order to have the captive licensed. Depending on the jurisdiction, the capital may be cash or, in some cases, an irrevocable letter of credit issued by a bank chartered in the state of domicile or a member bank of the Federal Reserve System.

The amount of capitalization required to start the captive varies by jurisdiction. Many will vary the amount depending on the structure of the captive (a pure captive may have a smaller capitalization requirement than an association captive). Typically, the capital required is $100,000 or more. In many cases, the amount set by statute may be increased by the insurance commissioner if he or she deems it advisable.

In addition to capital, a captive may have a surplus. Surplus is an insurance term. Assets of an insurance company are either *reserves* or *surplus*. Reserves are set aside to back the policies issued by the captives – in other words, set aside to pay potential claims. Surplus assets are everything else. Since reserves have an important function – paying possible claims – most jurisdictions place restrictions on how those assets may be invested. Not all assets can be claimed as meeting the jurisdiction's reserve requirement. Only certain assets, referred to as *permitted assets*, may be treated as reserves. The definition of permitted assets will depend on the laws of the domicile. For example, in some jurisdictions the value of real estate may be a permitted asset. In others, real estate is a permitted asset but only a certain percentage of its market value will be taken into account in determining whether the reserves requirement has been met.

The amount of reserves a captive needs is calculated by a qualified actuary familiar with the policies issued by the captive. These calculations are submitted to the insurance commissioner for review.

On the other hand, since surplus does not back future claims, there may be few if any investment restrictions on those amounts.

Investment policy

The investment policy set for the captive will be a function of the jurisdiction's laws regarding the investment of reserve funds, surplus funds and its definition of permitted assets as discussed above. It is important, of course, to work with an investment advisor familiar with not only the laws of the domicile selected by the captive but also familiar with prudent investment management. Often the investment policy is part of the business plan drawn up in the formation stage of the captive.

Reinsurance

Reinsurance is a simple enough concept – an insurance company *reinsures* its risks through another insurance company (i.e., passes on such risks to another insurer in return for paying a reinsurance premium to that insurer). A captive will reinsure some of its risks with a larger insurance company that has sufficient resources to cover a large claim should it occur.

Another reason why a captive seeks reinsurance is to properly distribute its risk. You will recall in an earlier chapter we discuss the fundamental definition of insurance. Insurance requires *risk shifting* and *risk distribution*. Risk shifting occurs when a business shifts its risk to the insurance company through an arm's length, properly drafted insurance policy. Risk shifting rests with the insured while, on the other hand, risk distribution rests with the insurance company. This makes sense because the concept behind insurance is taking advantage of the law of large numbers. Spreading a risk among thousands of policy holders helps ensure that a single claim will not bankrupt the insurance company. In other words, a true insurance company does not take on risk but distributes it among its policyholders.

The IRS requires such risk distribution for a captive to be treated as a valid insurance company. The IRS has ruled that a captive has sufficient distribution if (among other possible ways of satisfying this requirement) it receives more than 50% of its premium and risk from unrelated parties. In order to help their clients comply with this requirement, many captive managers have formed risk pools. The risk pool creates the pre-requisite diversification and helps a micro captive meet the IRS requirement.

A risk pool is a group of insurers or reinsurers through which particular types of risk are underwritten with premiums, losses, and expenses shared in agreed ratios. In rulings, the IRS has allowed these risk sharing pools to satisfy the risk diversification requirements.

A captive will join the risk pool, paying a premium and taking on certain responsibilities should a loss occur. For each member, claims paid bear a direct relationship to participating percentages. If your client's captive contributes .005% of the total pool premium it bears the same ratio on settled claims. Your client's adviser should make sure the pool goal is to:

- Ensure risk diversification; and
- Protect its members from a single claim that might cripple the pool.

But how does joining the pool help the captive meet the IRS rule that 50% of the captive's premiums must be from third parties? The captive pays a premium *to the pool* for the pool to take on some of the captive's risk. The captive then acts as a reinsurer – *it takes on some of the risk of the pool itself.* The captive gets paid to reinsure a portion of the risk the pool has taken on from all the captives in the pool. This is referred to as a *retrocessional pool.* Properly structured, 50% of the captive's premiums will be from third parties. Keep in mind – the captive is an insurance company and there is a risk that a large loss in the pool will result in a significant loss for all its members. Make sure your adviser is familiar with the pool he or she recommends. There should be strict underwriting and admission criteria.

A properly formed distribution pool will insure low frequency, high severity claims. The pool will contain many members (sometimes several hundred), all seeking risk diversification.

Independent Captive Associates, LLC: A Game Changer

ICA understands the importance of risk distribution pools. The structure and operation of the risk distribution pools needs to be understood by each captive owner to ensure each owner is comfortable with the risk being assumed, their obligations in the distribution pool and exit provisions. Unfortunately, most advisers fail to adequately explain the pros and cons of how risk distribution is accomplished. At ICA, communication is critical and never overlooked!

Reinsurance is crucial to the captive being recognized as an insurance company by the IRS. Make sure your client works with an adviser who fully understands risk distribution.

What You've Learned

Successfully implementing a micro captive is a systematic process that begins with a feasibility study and includes a business plan, pro forma financials and an actuarial study. In this chapter we took the process one step further, focusing on decisions that must be made on a number of key topics from ownership to reinsurance. In the next chapter we will discuss the licensing process and ongoing operations of the captive.

Chapter Seven

Nuts and Bolts II: Operations and Best Practices Going Forward

What you will learn: *The decision to go ahead with the captive has been made. The design and domicile issues have been settled. In this chapter you will learn about the licensing process and the day to day management of the captive. Care must be taken - all the work and money spent to form the captive and obtain the license will be wasted if the captive is not properly managed and operated as an independent insurance company. Because of the importance of the ongoing management of the captive, there is no final step to this process. That is why ongoing, professional management of the captive is so important to the overall success of the program.*

Once the domicile is selected, an application for an insurance license must be made. For the most part, the application process from domicile to domicile (especially the states) is similar. In fact, reading the statutes of the various states may lead you to conclude that the application process is identical. Compare the language in the captive laws of Vermont to the language in the South Carolina law regarding what the applicant must submit to the commissioner in regards to the ongoing management of the captive:

Vermont Law	South Carolina Law
(B) the adequacy of the expertise, experience, and character of the person or persons who will manage it; (C) the overall soundness of its plan of operation;	(B) the adequacy of the expertise, experience, and character of the person who will manage it; (C) the overall soundness of its plan of operation;

Ah, notice a slight similarity?

Setting aside the mirror-like laws, the quotes above tell us two things:

1. The states do tend to copy each other's legislation, so it is rare that one has a significant advantage over the other;

2. Domiciles *are* interested who will be responsible for the ongoing management of the captive, so select the ongoing manager of the captive with care!

There are, however, enough differences in the application process so you will want to make sure your adviser has experience applying for a license in the domicile you select. You will also take the same care in selecting the manager of the ongoing operations. It helps if the organization providing ongoing management is familiar to the commissioner's office.

In the next section we will look briefly at the application process in very general terms. An experienced adviser will be able to efficiently take your client through the specifics of the domicile selected.

IRC Section 501(c)(15) Captives

Occasionally an adviser will recommend that your client consider what is referred to as a Section 501(c) (15) captive. These were nonprofit insurance companies; Section 501 of the Internal Revenue Code lists corporations exempt from Federal income taxes. These nonprofit insurance companies paid no tax on any amount of investment income. Abuses of the 501(c) (15) code section lead Congress to make significant changes to the law in 2003. Now, the limits on the annual gross receipts earned by the 501(c) (15) to $350,000 with more than half having to come from premiums. These changes had the desired impact and limited the effectiveness of these entities for planning purposes. Any adviser making this recommendation is a little out of date!

The Application Process

The domicile will want to know:

- **Information about the captive your client is forming,** including the name, information on the number of shares being issued and initial capitalization. Recall that domiciles will require a minimum capitalization but the commissioner may increase it at his or her discretion. Most domiciles will also want to see copies of the Articles of Incorporation and company Bylaws. The application will also ask for the design and purpose of the captive.
- **Who are the captive's owners, directors and officers?** Anyone on the list who has a criminal record or recently declared

bankruptcy may result in the license being denied. There may also be questions on how much experience there is in the insurance business among the individuals named. A background check by a third party may be required.

- **What is the governance structure?** This includes naming the beneficial owners and how the board of directors will be elected, the function of the board (its authority and the policies and procedures of the board) and the election process of officers.
- **Ongoing management responsibility.** Who will have daily control and decision making authority?
- **Name of the service providers,** including the local firms involved. Typically a local auditor and insurance manager will be required. Other service providers include actuaries, lawyers, underwriters, etc.
- **The business plan.** We discussed this in detail in Chapter Five on the feasibility study. The commissioner may also require the actuarial study be submitted. The actuarial study explaining the coverage and limits will help the commissioner determine the capital requirements based on the risks insured and the loss analysis. In addition, the risk management and claims handling should be discussed. The actuarial study will also name the insureds. Recall that the domicile will issue a limited license to the captive. The commissioner will want to make sure the captive will not be issuing a policy to third parties. The business plan should also include the pro forma financial statements showing five years or more worth of projections.
- **Reinsurance** plans for the captive.
- **Investment policy** for reserves and surplus.
- **Will there be a fronting arrangement?** Fronting a reinsurance arrangement. In this case, the reinsurer is the captive. The captive arranges the issuance of an insurance policy through the "fronting company." The fronting company sells the policy, collects the premiums and administers the claims. The fronting company then shifts the risk to the captive through a reinsurance agreement. Why? There are several reasons, for example, the carrier must carry a minimum financial strength rating through an acceptable rating agency. Most captives do not have such a rating.

Along with the application, a check paying the application fee must be included. Finally, some domiciles request that the applicant demonstrate that issuing the license will be of benefit to the local economy. This Certificate of Public Good provides information on the number of local jobs that will be created in the domicile and the estimated amount of deposits that will be made in local financial institutions.

Depending on the domicile, there may be a required meeting with the insurance commissioner. In some domiciles, the interview may be completed by the local insurance manager who may also hand deliver the application. In other jurisdictions the meeting may have to include the owners of the captive.

Ongoing Operations

Your client must keep in mind that a real insurance company is being established and that it must operate independently. Large or small, the captive must be operated properly. *Courts will look to see if the captive was operating as a fully functioning, independent corporation in order to determine if it was a legitimate insurance company. The IRS will not recognize the deductibility of premiums paid to the captive if it is not operated as a standalone business.* Failure to operate the captive successfully will mean all the time, effort and money spent on the design, implementation and licensing of the captive will have been wasted. Further, all that your client hoped to accomplish with the captive in the future will fail to be realized.

This means that the company your client hires to handle the day to day operation of the captive must have a successful track record and demonstrate deep experience operating an insurance company. Like any other insurance company, the captive issues insurance policies, pays claims and must maintain reserves. The captive maintains a separate set of books and has separate management. It must keep its operations at arms-length from those of its owners and members of the same affiliated group.

It also must be careful to operate within the constraints of its limited insurance license.

What You've Learned

We've come a long way since we first raised the topic of captive insurance companies at the beginning of our book. We hope you took our advice and introduced the micro captive insurance company idea to your clients. Each step along the way must be done carefully and preferably with the assistance of an experienced adviser. From the feasibility study to managing the day to day operations of the captive, there are pitfalls that only an experienced adviser can help you avoid. We believe the time, effort and money invested to establish a captive will benefit your client in two important ways. The first is as a tremendous risk management tool. The second is as a means to create, preserve and transfer wealth. We turn to that topic in the next chapter.

Chapter Eight

Wealth Creation, Preservation and Transfer

What you will learn: *Federal estate and gift taxes (transfer taxes) can consume $.40 of every dollar your wealthiest clients hope to transfer to their loved ones. While the passage of the American Taxpayer Relief Act (ATRA) of 2012 increased both the estate tax exemption and the lifetime gift tax exemption, it also increased the estate tax rate to 40% for anyone with an estate in excess of the exemption. In addition to Federal transfer taxes, many states have become more aggressive in recent years collecting estate taxes and these state taxes must also be carefully considered in your client's planning. Fortunately, the implementation of a micro-captive can help your client create substantial wealth for its owners – wealth that can be preserved and transferred to heirs without the imposition of transfer taxes. In this chapter we will briefly summarize the income tax benefits of captives we discussed earlier in our book, the wealth creation possibilities of a micro-captive insurance company and how to preserve and transfer those gains to your client's loved ones.*

Wealth creation begins with running a profitable captive insurance company. While the tax benefits we discuss below are important to understand, tax benefits by themselves will not help your client create wealth if the captive is poorly designed, implemented or operated. *And if you don't create wealth, there is nothing to preserve or transfer.*

We reviewed the Federal income tax benefits of micro-captives in Chapter Three. In this chapter we are going to take a look at the Federal estate and gift tax (*or transfer taxes*) planning opportunities that can make it possible for your client to pass on considerable wealth to his or her heirs without the imposition of transfer taxes. *While the Federal income tax benefits of captives help with wealth creation, proper estate and gift tax planning with captives assists with wealth preservation and transfer.*

Unfortunately, we have found most often that those who understand the use of captives primarily as a risk management tool do not understand income, gift and estate tax law. And those who understand income, gift and estate tax law do not understand captives! Somehow that gap must be bridged. Your client's tax situation is unique; there is no "cookie cutter" approach that will work for everyone.

If you are not your client's attorney, you will want to make sure your client's estate planning attorney is involved early in the process of creating and implementing a captive. Your independent captive adviser must be able to bridge the "knowledge gap" between your client's attorney and the wealth creation, preservation and transfer opportunities available with a micro-captive.

A full discussion of Federal estate and gift tax planning is beyond the scope of this book. Our goal is to give you enough information to enable you to hold a basic discussion on this topic with your client. We also want you to have enough information to ask questions of the captive adviser and understand their responses. In some cases, you may find the adviser unfamiliar with some of these tax provisions (in that case, your client may want to find another adviser).

Tax Benefits Table

In the table below, we summarize the Federal income, gift and estate tax implications of establishing a micro-captive insurance company. Notice we list the benefits for all the parties involved: the sponsoring (or insured) company which may or not own the captive, the micro-captive insurance company itself, the shareholders of the captive and finally, the shareholders of the sponsoring company.

Sponsoring (or Insured) Company	Micro-Captive Insurance Company	Shareholders of Captive	Shareholders of Sponsoring (or Insured) Company
• *Tax deductions for premiums paid** • *The ability to deduct the premium payment while, at the same time, shifting tax free income to the micro-captive electing IRC Section 831(b) will lower the overall marginal tax rates paid by both entities (effectively, you are moving up to $1,200,000 in premium income to a 0% tax rate)** • *At a 40% Federal and state income tax rate, the tax savings can be as much as $480,000 (or 40% times $1.2 million)**	• *If IRC Section 831(b) election is made, no taxation of premium income** • *Investment income will be taxed at lower marginal tax rate due to the exclusion of the premium income**	• *As untaxed premium income accrues year after year in the captive, the value of the captive is increasing for shareholders** • *Any distributions of dividends may be taxed at favorable rates depending upon the law at the time of distribution* • *Redemptions of stock at time of retirement or other triggering event should result in capital gain income which is currently subject to favorable levels of taxation* • *The shares of the captive may be held in trust for the benefit of adult children; this protects the shares from the claims of the children's creditors*	• *Assets represented by the premiums paid annually are transferred to family members or their trusts without transfer taxes* • *If captive is held by trusts, the shareholders of the sponsor may be named as trustees without estate tax inclusion*

****Discussed in Chapter Three.***

There are other benefits to a captive insurance company unrelated to taxes – such as asset protection and use of captive shares as an executive deferred compensation plan – that we do not discuss in this book but that may be viable strategies for your client. An added advantage of using captives for deferred compensation strategies is that the captive need not seek approval from the U.S. Department of Labor or comply with ERISA (but consult with your attorney before proceeding with these types of plans).

Wealth Creation

If actual claims experience is favorable, the captive will show a profit for the owner(s), which can be accumulated, distributed as dividends, or paid out to shareholders upon liquidation.

You may recall that early on we noted that Warren Buffett loves the insurance business. Why? Let's take a look at his most recent letter to shareholders recapping the financial results:

> "Berkshire's extensive insurance operation again operated at an underwriting profit in 2013 – that makes 11 years in a row – and increased its float. During that 11 year stretch, our float – money that doesn't belong to us but that we can invest for Berkshire's benefit – has grown from $41 billion to $77 billion…And all of this all began with our 1967 purchase of National Indemnity for $8.6 million."

In particular, Buffet likes Property and Casualty (P/C) insurers which *"…receive premiums upfront and pay claims later…This collect now, pay-later model leaves P/C companies holding large sums – money we call 'float' – that will eventually go to others. Meanwhile, insurers get to invest this float for their benefit."*

Of course, the comparison between a micro captive, larger captives and publicly traded insurance companies (such as Berkshire) is not exact and can only go so far. For one reason, the micro captive has a better tax benefit with the $1,200,000 annual premium exclusion from income. But the point is this: as premiums are paid into the micro captive, investment income, although taxed annually, grows and accumulates along with the tax free premium income that builds up year after year. This is a powerful tool for wealth creation. As we mention in the table above, moving up to $1,200,000 from the sponsoring company to the captive can save up to $480,000 in Federal and state income taxes if the sponsoring company's combined tax rate is 40%. If properly planned, this money also avoids transfer taxes.

During its operation, the cumulative tax benefits help create long term wealth. It is true that this wealth will eventually be taxed when distributed as dividends or the shareholders sell their shares and recognize capital gains. But this may be many years away and then, as now, there may be favorable tax rates on qualified dividends and long term capital gains.

Some commentators compare a captive to a *family bank* that accepts deposits (the premium payments) and earns income on its invested premiums but does not have to pay interest to depositors. Of course, a bank does not have to pay claims on insurable losses as a captive does, but you get the picture. Run well, the micro captive takes in a lot of cash and pays out few claims and builds wealth over the years.

This all begins to look good even after the start up and ongoing operating costs are taken into account.

But, you ask, what about transfer taxes? How can proper planning with a captive reduce potential transfer taxes imposed at a 40% Federal tax rate (not including state estate taxes)?

Wealth Preservation and Transfer: Avoiding or Minimizing Federal Estate and Gift Tax

In this section we will focus on *Federal* estate and gift taxes. Make sure, however, your client's tax advisor and/or estate planning attorney does not overlook *state* estate and gift taxes. Depending on the state your client lives (and dies) in state estate and gift taxes can be significant. States have become more aggressive in recent years imposing these taxes.

The Federal estate tax is applied to the assets the decedent leaves behind in his "taxable estate." He or she may leave as much as $5,340,000 in 2014 without imposition of the estate tax. *This is known as the estate tax exemption.* It is adjusted annually for inflation. The decedent may use up only a portion of the exemption. For example, Joe dies in 2014 with a taxable estate of $2,000,000. That means he will not have used $3,340,000 of his estate tax exemption. That unused portion may be passed on to his spouse. Her estate tax exemption will be $8,680,000 (or $5,340,000 minus $2,000,000 used by Joe plus her estate tax exemption of $5,340,000). Of course, if Joe used none of his estate tax exemption at the time of his passing, he and his spouse could pass on as much as $10,680,000 exempt from estate tax. Anything over that would be subject to the 40% estate tax rate.

Independent Captive Associates, LLC: A Game Changer

ICA has expertise in all areas of captive design, formation and operation. In addition, we are strong in business integration services from succession planning to estate planning. We are not a law firm. We work closely, however, with our clients' legal counsel to make sure the captive is fully and properly integrated with his or her estate plan. We can offer planning ideas and review documents prepared by the attorney.

For you wealthiest clients, $.40 of every dollar will go to estate taxes once their estate value exceeds the exemption. This does not count state estate taxes or inheritance taxes if applicable (often confused, an estate tax is <u>not</u> the same as an inheritance tax; an inheritance tax applies and is paid by the individual inheriting or receiving the bequest; the estate tax applies and is paid from the taxable estate the decedent left behind). To complicate matters, your clients may be subject to the Generation-Skipping Transfer (GST) taxes and gift taxes that also limit their ability to transfer property to their family members (even family members not yet born!) without incurring these *transfer* taxes.

Gift taxes apply to transfers made by your client while alive. Unfortunately, your client cannot avoid the estate tax just by giving your assets away while alive. But your client can avoid paying the gift tax by:

- Giving away only $14,000 per year per donee. If you client has five children and six grandchildren, he can give away $154,000 (or 11 donees times $14,000). He and his wife can each give $14,000 per year per donee. This would allow them to transfer gifts with a value of $308,000 without transfer taxes).
- Using up his or her lifetime gift tax exemption of $5,340,000. If your client, a widower who has not remarried, gave his son a $100,000 gift in 2014 the excess is $86,000 (or $100,000 minus $14,000). When filing his gift tax return for 2014 he applies $86,000 against his lifetime gift tax exemption. That means his lifetime exemption is now $5,254,000 (or $5,340,000 minus $86,000). But here's the catch: use of the lifetime gift tax exemption also reduces his estate tax exemption by $86,000.

> The estate tax and gift tax work together. While no gift tax will be due in 2014, both his lifetime gift tax exemption and estate tax exemption are reduced.

Now, rather than transferring $100,000 to his son which reduces his transfer tax exemptions, with a captive your client can now transfer up to $1,200,000 out of his or her future estate without incurring any transfer taxes. Nor does your client have to "dip in" to his transfer tax exemption because of the payment of premiums to the captive. But it takes careful estate planning to accomplish this, so caution must be exercised.

We can provide you a basic example of how this works below. A knowledgeable estate planning attorney (meaning one who understands estate planning *and* captive insurance companies!) will create a structure that fits your client's specific circumstances and estate planning needs.

The most basic structure would have the captive shares held in a trust for the benefit of your client's adult children. The captive in this case is referred to as a *CHIC or closely-held insurance company*. At the time the gift of stock is made to the trust there is no taxable gift – the value of the shares in the CHIC are nominal at that point. Once established, up to $1,200,000 in wealth can be transferred annually to the captive. The beneficiaries of the trust will benefit from all future growth in the value of the CHIC. Had the captive not been established, the premiums would have been left in the insured company. This growth in value absent the captive would eventually be subject to transfer taxes. But assets represented by the payment of the insurance premiums transferred to the captive will build in value over the years not subject to transfer taxes at the death of the parent. At the time the CHIC shares are sold, special capital gains tax rates may apply that will further lower the marginal tax rates paid on the entire transaction – from the formation of the captive to the final liquidation.

Transfer planning techniques are always being refined and updated as the estate tax laws change. In addition, your client's personnel circumstances may change (divorce, death, etc.), which may require changing the estate plan. Make sure your client updates his or her estate tax plan at least every few years.

What You've Learned

The benefits of a micro-captive insurance company are wide ranging: improved risk management, a variety of tax benefits, wealth creation, preservation and transfer. In this chapter we discussed how proper estate and gift tax planning can result in transferring the wealth to your family members without the imposition of transfer taxes that can take as much as 40% of every dollar your client hoped to leave to his or her loved ones. But proceed carefully – make sure you are working with professional advisers who understand captive insurance companies as well as sophisticated estate and gift tax planning techniques that will be implemented by attorneys.

Chapter Nine

Pulling It All Together: A Real Life Case Study

What you will learn: *In this chapter we pull it all together in a case study. In our book, you've covered all aspects of the micro captive insurance company strategy from the basic concepts to design, implementation and operation. Now with this case study you will see how all of it fits together. Maybe your "ah-ha moment" came early in our book. Maybe your "ah-ha moment" will come after you read the case study. Either way, we think you will agree with us that, for the right client, a micro-captive strategy is an excellent risk management and wealth enhancing tool.*

An adviser from Independent Captive Associates, LLC meets with Chris Rone. The adviser has been called in by Chris' longtime business adviser and accountant. The accountant heard about captive insurance companies during a presentation and is convinced that Chris would be a good fit. The ICA adviser, the accountant and Chris sat down to discuss the situation. This is what the adviser learned.

Chris Rone is 40 years old with substantial net worth. Chris is the sole owner of a hedge fund, Gemini Assets. After employee bonuses, Gemini has $2.5 million of taxable income. The combined tax rate (Federal, state and local) is 51% meaning - Chris' "take home" was $1,225,000 after tax bills of $1,275,000.

Gemini manages four different investment strategies: a long-short equity fund, a convertible arbitrage fund, a distressed debt fund, and a multi-strategy fund-of-funds. The fund has a domestic and offshore fund that feed into a master feeder-fund. Gemini also owns two separate real estate entities in two separate locations.

Chris is married and has three children. Chris knows that with $40,000,000 in assets, estate and gift taxes will take a big bite out of the estate left behind for the children. It is time for some serious planning to minimize transfer taxes. In addition, Chris would like to reduce current income tax liability and accumulate assets on a more tax advantaged basis.

As it turns out, Chris is an *ideal candidate* for a captive insurance company. Independent Captive Associates, LLC is hired to provide advice and guidance. ICA performs a feasibility study, analyzing Gemini's current coverage to determine risks that are either self-insured or under-insured. The risks identified are listed in the table below, along with the premiums and coverage limits.

Risks Identified –Type of Coverage*	Annual Premium	Coverage Limit
State or Federal Legislative Changes *If Gemini were no longer allowed to sell its investment funds due to change in state or federal legislation risk.*	$220,000	$1,250,000 annually; $2,000,000 Limit of Liability
Directors and Officers Liability *D & O exposed to litigation and liability risk.*	$150,000	$212,000 annually; $250,000 Limit of Liability
Market Volatility *Operates in unstable investment environment, revenue tied to its investment performance.*	$150,000	$1,000,000 annually; $2,000,000 Limit of Liability
Inability of Insured Employee to Work *Company cannot operate at high level if key employee is unable to work.*	$100,000	$87,500 annually; $435,000 Limit of Liability
Business Litigation Matters *Litigious business environment, expense and distraction of a large law suit can result in loss of revenue.*	$100,000	$200,000 annually; $400,000 Limit of Liability
Tax Audit Defense or Tax Controversy *Hedge fund companies draw close scrutiny by IRS. Losses due to adverse tax ruling could be costly.*	$14,000	$50,000 annually; $100,000 Limit of Liability

Computer System Failure Caused by Detrimental Code *Trading strategies rely heavily on computer driven quantitative methods and technology. Inability to use systems even for a short time would be extremely costly.*	$100,000	$150,000 annually; $500,000 Limit of Liability
Data Breach Liability *A date breach of confidential client data would incur significant operating and financial risks.*	$196,000	$290,000 annually; $380,000 Limit of Liability
Changes in U.S. Tax Laws *Tax environment is uncertain; adverse changes would expose hedge fund managers to significant losses.*	$65,000	$100,000 annually; $200,000 Limit of Liability
Loss of Significant Client *Many of company's clients come through private placement resulting in a few very large clients; the loss of any would create a substantial loss in revenue and income.*	$55,000	$110,000 annually; $225,000 Limit of Liability
Total Annual Premiums	**$1,150,000**	N/A

*<u>Note:</u>

- **All coverage was determined to be appropriate risks to insure.**
- Named insured under all policies: **Gemini Assets**
- All coverage: **12 month term**
- Coverage trigger: **All claims made during the coverage period**
- All coverage: **$0 deductible**
- Coverage territory: **USA and Cayman Islands**

The recommended annual premiums of $1,150,000 are determined by application of usual and customary insurance underwriting principles. The premiums are believed to be reasonable in relation to the benefits provided without regard to any experience based premium refund or benefit. Chris accepts ICA's recommendation and decides to move ahead. After careful consideration, ICA recommends that the captive be licensed in Kentucky.

After conducting a study to determine the proper risk shifting/distribution necessary to submit a study to the state insurance department, Chris creates, with ICA's guidance, a captive insurance company in Kentucky called *Hedge Insurance Company* ("Hedge"). The captive meets the IRC Section 831(b) rules to be treated as a micro captive insurance company. ICA will perform the captive's administrative operations through its arrangement with a captive manager.

The shares of the captive will be owned by three trusts for the benefit of Chris' children. Chris and spouse will act as trustees. The captive will not be subject to the claims of Chris' personal creditors. Furthermore, transfers of the shares will not be part of Chris' (or the spouse's) taxable estate nor will it be considered a gift for Federal gift tax purposes.

The state of Kentucky approved the business plan and issued the necessary insurance license, and Gemini has operated its captive successfully since 2007.

Benefits: This hedge fund small captive strategy delivers several significant tax benefits to Chris:

- The premiums paid by Gemini to the captive are fully deductible for income tax purposes. At a 51% tax rate, the income tax savings are $586,500 annually (51% times $1,150,000).
- Due to the IRC Section 831(b) election, the captive will not be taxed on premium income, but only on the investment income it earns.
- Under current tax law, a captive generates favorable tax distributions in the form of favorable tax rates on capital gains and qualified dividends. Compared to Chris' current tax rate of 51% this will create a large and favorable arbitrage.
- The state insurance department approved the micro captive's surplus being invested in the hedge fund manager's funds at a lower tax rate than the hedge fund manager's own tax bracket.
- The captive and its assets will not be subject to the claims of the hedge fund creditor for asset protection purposes.
- The captive and all of its future growth can be arranged so that it will not be part of the hedge fund manager's taxable estate. Chris' children's trust will maintain significant assets outside of Chris' (and spouse's) taxable estate.

What You've Learned

If you go back to the beginning of this chapter and review Chris' goals, you'll find that the micro captive strategy met them all – and more. Chris not only reduced current income taxes, future estate and gift taxes were also reduced substantially. In addition, the captive strategy offered asset protection features that Chris did not set out to achieve as a goal, but that he appreciated as the plan was implemented. You can create the same value for your clients that Chris realized.

Appendix

Appendix: Key Case Rulings and IRS Authority

Here is a partial list of the authority that governs captive insurance companies:

Court Cases

Name	Summary
Helvering v. LaGriese, 312 U.S. 531 (1941)	U.S. Supreme Court defines insurance as comprising of risk shifting and risk distribution
Crawford Fitting Co. v. U.S. (1985)	Established that insurance premiums paid to a captive by a group of separate corporations that were owned by a group of related individuals were deductible because the shareholder/policyholders of the captive were not so economically related that their separate financial transactions had to be aggregated and treated as the transactions of a single taxpayer.
Humana, Inc. v. Commissioner, 881 F.2nd 247 (1989)	Court rejects use of "economic family doctrine"
Harper Group and Includable Subsidiaries v. Commissioner, 96 T.C. 45 (1992)	Court rejects IRS contention that no risk shifting exists where a parent pays premium to a subsidiary to insure conduct of its business.
Rent-A-Center vs. Commissioner, 142 T.C. No. 1 (Jan. 14, 2014)	IRS overruled by Tax Court which found the captive was a bona fide insurance company despite the existence of an agreement between the parent and the captive. The parent guaranteed the captive's liabilities up to $25 million.

IRS Revenue Rulings

Ruling	Summary
77-316	The IRS adopts the "economic family doctrine" stating that premiums paid by a parent to a subsidiary are not deductible.
2001-31	IRS abandons the "economic family doctrine" acquiescing to a series of court decisions. Establishes a facts and circumstances test to determine if the captive is an insurance company.
2002-89; 2002-90; 2002-91	IRS issues safe harbors to help taxpayers determine if adequate risk distribution was achieved by the captive.
2005-40	IRS states that risk distribution is not met if the captive insures only one entity.
2014-15	Permits companies to use captives to fund retiree health benefits without having to obtain a PLR if it meets certain requirements.

IRS Revenue Procedures

Revenue Procedure	Summary
2002-75	IRS removes captive insurance transactions from the list of transactions for which rulings and determination letters will not be ordinarily issued.

IRS Private Letter Rulings

In the PLRs below, the IRS responds to taxpayer requests regarding the structure of their captive insurance transactions and whether the arrangement between the insureds and the captives constitutes insurance for federal income tax purposes.

200907006

200950016

200950017

201030014

201126036

201219011